Published in 2023
by Vision Australia
454 Glenferrie Road,
Kooyong, Victoria 3144

Produced by
Berbay Publishing
PO Box 133
Kew East
Victoria 3102

Vision Australia gratefully acknowledges
the generous support from The Elliot Family Trust.

Printed in China

National Library of Australia
Cataloguing-in-publication data:
Dickson, John
Craig Shanahan: Cooking Up a Storm

For primary school children
ISBN 978-0-6455584-1-8

CRAIG SHANAHAN

COOKING UP A STORM

Written by John Dickson
Illustrated by Claudia Frittitta

When Craig was born, his mum noticed that one of his eyes looked a bit odd. When Craig was two years old, a doctor told his mother that Craig had cancer in his left eye. The treatment he needed meant Craig spent a lot of time in hospital. After a while, the doctors decided his eye had to be removed. By the time he was five years old, Craig had only one eye.

At school, other kids would ask Craig, 'What's it like to have one eye?' Craig would answer, 'What's it like to have two?' Craig likes to be funny. Having one eye was all he knew. It made no difference to him. He could read, write and draw pictures like everybody else in his class. He could ride a bike, run and swim.

In high school, Craig had lots of friends. Other kids liked him because he was friendly and very funny. The friends he made then are still his friends now. Craig's favourite subject was food technology.

This taught him where food comes from, which foods are good for you and how to cook them. Craig decided to become a chef.

Craig went to college to study more about cooking. After six months, he was offered an apprenticeship. Craig loves to learn new things. He also works very hard.

BAKING

In his early years as an apprentice chef, Craig would work at three different kitchens every week. He would begin his day at six o'clock in the morning. Often, he would not be finished until eleven o'clock that night. Then he would get up the next morning and do it all over again. Six days a week.

Craig learned how to cook many different dishes, from simple hamburgers to fancy meals in a posh restaurant. He even worked for a famous TV chef.

After a few years, Craig was feeling a bit tired. He decided to have a break and move to Queensland to be with his brother. He became more and more tired. Sometimes, he could not even finish his dinner before he needed to go to sleep.

His brother noticed that Craig's right eye looked a bit odd. His mum visited from Sydney and said he should go to a doctor. Immediately.

The doctors took a special picture of Craig's brain. They found something that shouldn't be there. It was a growth the size of a mango and it was pressing up against his good eye. It had to come out. After the operation to remove the growth, Craig was almost completely blind.

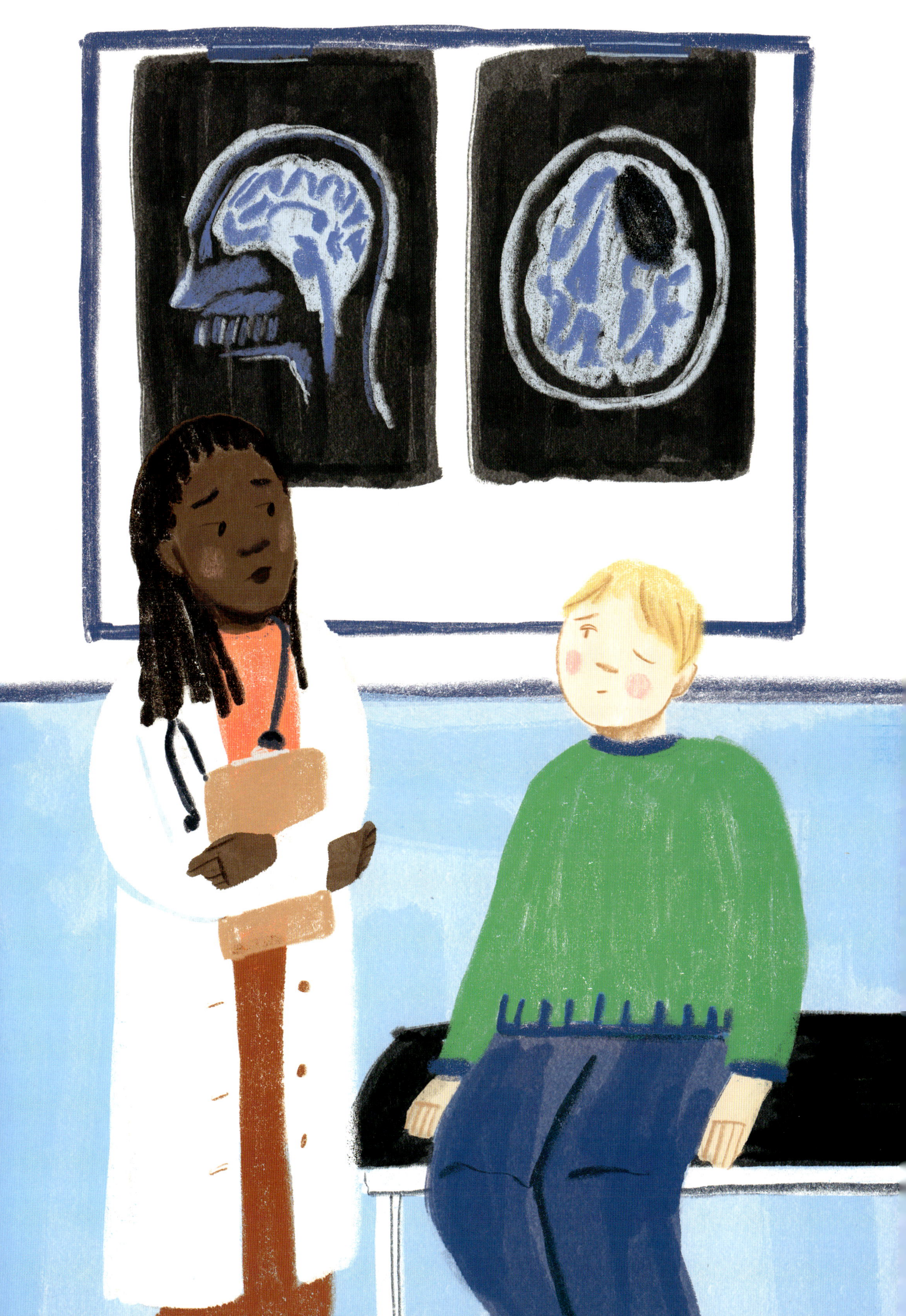

It took Craig a long time to recover. Before he could leave hospital, he had to learn how to walk again. This time with a cane. He also developed some superpowers: he could smell better than ever, he could hear people talking from a long way away, and touching things told him amazing secrets.

Sometimes, Craig would feel sad about being blind. But not for long. There were things he wanted to do, so he decided that being blind was not going to stop him. Back home in Sydney, Craig worked even harder at getting better and stronger.

He knew he had to. He had a dream.
Craig wanted to open his own café.

When he couldn't get the money to pay for the café, his schoolmates and his friends on the internet stepped in to help. Soon, it was time to open the doors. Craig named his café The Blind Chef Café and Dessert Bar.

THE BLIND CHEF

Everybody is welcome at Craig's café. He carefully designed it so that disabled people could bring their wheelchairs and blind people could bring their Seeing Eye Dogs. Other dogs are welcome, too. As long as they are well behaved.

Craig has a Seeing Eye Dog named Rocko. Rocko goes everywhere with Craig. Sometimes, if he has been good, he is allowed to sleep on Craig's bed. When you go to Craig's café, Rocko will be there to greet you and get a pat.

Craig's café is fun. You might be invited to put on a blindfold and eat a four-course meal while you are 'blind'. There are prizes for guessing what food is on the plate. And there are prizes for eating the entire meal without using your fingers!

Sometimes, you can go into the kitchen and watch Craig cook a three-course meal.

Craig loves his café and he is very proud of what he has achieved. He says he is lucky to have the support of all the people who have helped him, especially his family.

Craig says, 'I know there are many people a lot worse off than me. They inspire me to work hard and do the things I want to do. Being blind will not stop me!'

GLOSSARY

Cancer

A disease that happens when cells in our body become abnormal and grow and spread out of control. They can stop the body's good cells from doing their job and can lead to very serious health issues.

Seeing Eye Dog

A Seeing Eye Dog has been trained to lead a blind person, helping them to have independence.

Walking with a cane

People who are blind or vision impaired can sometimes use a white cane to help them find obstacles in their way when they are walking. It also helps other people know that the user is blind or vision impaired and to take care.